3rd Edition
The Christian
BABYSITTER'S HANDBOOK

Written by Sarah Fletcher • Edited by Melinda Walz

CONCORDIA PUBLISHING HOUSE • SAINT LOUIS

For all baby-sitters WHO love their jobs

Copyright © 2006 Concordia Publishing House
3558 S. Jefferson Avenue
St. Louis, MO 63118-3968
1-800-325-3040 • www.cph.org

Written by Sarah Fletcher
Edited by Melinda Walz
Cover illustration by Debra Spina Dixon

Scripture quotations are from The Holy Bible, English Standard Version, copyright © 2001 by Crossway Bibles, a division of Good News Publishers. Used by permission. All rights reserved.

This publication may be available in braille, in large print, or on cassette tape for the visually impaired. Please allow 8 to 12 weeks for delivery. Write to the Library for the Blind, 7550 Watson Rd., St. Louis, MO 63119-4409; call 1-866-215-6852; or e-mail to blind.mission@blindmission.org.

Manufactured in the United States of America

Library of Congress Cataloging-in-Publication Data

Fletcher, Sarah

    The Christian babysitter's handbook/Sarah Fletcher.—New ed.
        p.   cm.
    Originally published: St. Louis: Concordia, 1985.
    ISBN 0-570-04889-3
    1. Baby-sitting—Handbooks, manuals, etc.—Juvenile literature.

    2. Baby-sitters—Juvenile literature. 3. Youth—Religious life—Juvenile literature.
4. Christian education of children—Juvenile literature. I. Title.
HQ769.5.F54 1997
649'.1'0248—dc20   96-43745

1 2 3 4 5 6 7 8 9 10   15 14 13 12 11 10 09 08 07 06

Contents

Contents

Contents

CHAPTER 1

So, You're a Christian Babysitter. . .

How do you feel about that?

Maybe you've never babysat before. In that case, your stomach may feel a little like an elevator without any brakes. That's understandable. After all, you're suddenly switching roles in a big way. Until now, other people have been taking care of you. Now you're the one who will be taking care of others.

What kind of pictures do you see in your mind? Long, empty hours you somehow have to fill before you can put the kids to bed? A huge, creaky house with prowlers peeking through every window and emergencies lurking around every corner? Or, are you remembering all the things you used to do to your own babysitters? (Be honest; your sins will find you out!) Don't worry. The pages ahead will give you some ideas not only for filling those long hours, but also for making them good ones for both you and the children. You'll read about handling emergencies, too—should any emerge. You might even learn a trick or two that your babysitters didn't know.

Then again, maybe you aren't nervous at all. Maybe you've babysat a lot in the past and are frankly just a little bored with the whole thing. Read on anyway. A fresh outlook might help you, and there's no better way to get one than to realize that what you're doing is honest-to-goodness Christian ministry.

That brings us to the key question.

Does being a Christian babysitter make any Difference?

Does it ever! It makes a difference in how you feel about the kids, how you feel about what you're doing, and how you feel about you. In fact, as God's Holy Spirit helps you celebrate the fact that Jesus gave His life to win you new life, being a Christian makes a difference in your whole life—including babysitting.

11

CHAPTER 2

WHat's Babysitting?

Well, it doesn't always mean babies.
Sometimes you'll be taking care of older
kids—and you'd better not call them babies, at
least not when they can hear you. Babysitting
usually doesn't mean sitting, either.
Sometimes—like when you're giving Michael
his 14th horsey ride or fishing around under
the king-size bed for Ashley's lost teddy bear—
you'll wish you *could* do a little more sitting.

No, what "babysitting" means is that for a period of time, you are responsible for the lives of one or more of God's children. When parents leave their kids in your care, it's a giant leap of faith for them. They trust you to do the important job of caring for their children—they trust you to do the best job you can and to keep the kids safe.

Does that sound like serious stuff? It is. But that doesn't mean babysitting can't be fun—and rewarding, too.

Before we get to the fun and rewards, though, think for a moment about the word **responsible**. It comes from the word **respond**. You must be able to respond to the needs of the children you're watching. You must be

able to respond to their parents' expectation that you'll do a good job. And you must be able to respond to God's will for you.

How did God get into all this? That's simple. He has called you—and all other Christians—to actively serve Him. It's right there in 1 Peter:

"But you are a chosen race, a royal priesthood, a holy nation, a people for His own possession, that you may proclaim the excellencies of Him who called you out of darkness into His marvelous Light." (1 Peter 2:9)

Being God's servant is a full-time job. It gets mixed up in every part of your life. It means that you serve God by serving His people—including the children you babysit.

Now, just because you're a responsible child of God doesn't mean you have to go around looking like a moldy prune. It doesn't mean you have to march around like a five-star general, either. You can be responsible and have fun too. You can play with the kids and laugh at their silliness. You can even get pretty silly yourself. But at the same time, one part of you must always remember: **I'm in charge here. I've got to be on top of things— all the time.**

Sometimes being responsible may even mean saying no to a job. If you know that you're getting in over your head, maybe saying no or asking if a responsible adult can come along is the best bet. If you've never changed a diaper and you're asked to sit for a two-year old and newborn twins, being responsible means asking for help.

If you can balance those two things—responsibility and fun—then babysitting will bring you rewards that are even better than the money you'll earn. You might get a phone call from a parent who says, "can you come next Friday night? we'd rather have you than anyone else." Or you might be tucking in a cover and suddenly hear a sleepy little voice say, "I love you." Or, best of all, you might know that special feeling deep inside that comes when God is saying to you, **"Servant, well done!"**

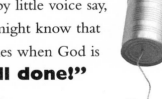

CHAPTER 3

Getting a Job
(If That's the Issue)

If it isn't your problem, if you've got as many babysitting jobs as you can handle, skip this chapter or consider starting your own sitters' agency. (It's been done before. What you do is promise to provide responsible sitters for parents who need them—and jobs for responsible sitters. Then you either charge the parents a small fee or take a small percentage of what the sitters earn. Again, though, the key word is responsible.)

But suppose you are responsible, ready, and eager to babysit, and no one asks you. How can you make the phone start ringing? Fear not. Your condition is temporary. The parents with jobs to offer are out there, and they're probably as ready and eager as you are.

The secret is to let them know you're there. Nobody's going to buy a super new invention if it's hidden away in a warehouse some- where. And nobody's going to hire the services of a sitter they don't know has those services to sell. So stop hiding your light under a bushel. **Advertise!** You might start by talking to friends who already do a lot of babysitting. Ask them to recommend you for the jobs they can't take. Ask your parents, relatives, and friends to mention your new career to their friends, too.

Make a list of neighbors with small children. Then give them each a call or hand them each a flyer to tell them you're going into business. Parents usually like having a sitter in the neighborhood. It makes transportation so much easier.

It's not a bad idea to do some volunteer work with kids, either. It gives you the opportunity to get some valuable experience. It also gives parents the chance to see how great you are with their kids. Helping in the church nursery, with Vacation Bible School, or at Sunday school are good places to start.

You may also consider taking a babysitting class. It can help you prepare for the job and can be a great advertising point. It shows parents you are serious about the business of babysitting and about taking care of their kids. The nearest hospital likely has babysitting classes. And the American Red Cross has a really good program to help new babysitters get started. If those two sources don't work, consider asking your church to offer a babysitting training course or workshop.

Another effective way to advertise is by putting a card on the bulletin board at your church. (Be sure to get permission from the church office or your pastor before you do this, though.) Keep the card simple—and neat. A brightly colored border around the card wouldn't hurt, either. If you have good computer skills, or know someone who does, you can design and print your own simple business cards. That makes it even easier for you to hand out—and for potential customers to take—your information.

With all that advertising and with a little patience, you should soon have all the sitting jobs you can handle.

When you advertise that you're available for babysitting jobs, you will want to let people know that you're up to the job. Ask a couple of your teachers, your scout leader, or other adults who know you to write letters of recommendation. (Don't ask your own parents or grandparents to write recommendations, though.) Put the words **"references available"** on the card you post on the church bulletin board or on your business cards. Then, when you're talking to people who ask you about babysitting, ask if they'd like to see your letters of recommendation.

Don't be surprised if parents interview you. After all, it's a job. And when it comes to their kids, parents are pretty protective. Some parents will ask you questions about your interests, what kind of student you are, and how you would respond to things. This is a way they can get to know you and decide if you're the right sitter for their kids. Other parents will ask questions of people who know you. They might do a background check by calling your references or by calling other families you've babysat for to find out how well you've done other jobs.

This isn't about you—it's about their children. Parents won't hire just anyone to take care of their kids, so if they ask you to be their babysitter, it means they trust you and they like you.

CHAPTER 4

Here I Am!

It's come at last—that first babysitting job. Or perhaps it's just your first job with a new family. In either case, you walk in the door and see a dressed-up adult or two smiling at you. You see a couple of wide-eyed children peering at you.

What do they see when you walk in the door? A girl with purple hair or a boy in ripped jeans? A kid with the posture of a limp pretzel or with elbows poking out of the world's oldest sweatshirt?

True, on the inside you are a beautiful person, but facts are also facts. And it's a fact that when you're making a first impression, **outsides matter**—a lot. Of course you don't have to dress as if you're about to enter a corporate boardroom, but you don't have to look like a refugee from a horror film, either. Wear something clean and neat—something that makes you look like the responsible person you are.

Then there's the matter of **manners**. A polite "Yes, ma'am" or "No, sir" never hurt anyone. Good manners also make adults think like this: "H-m-m-m. Obviously that kid has been well raised. A kid like that should do a good job with our kids." Besides, good manners really are linked to the heart. Manners are a way of

Here I Am!

acting out how we feel about people, and that's a way of living out the love God gives to us in Jesus.

Finally, there's **attitude**. You've got one and it's good. You're serving God's people, and you're going to do the best, most responsible job you can. So how can you help the family you're working for see that? Well, attitudes are partly communicated through the things we've already mentioned—dress, posture, manners. But there are other ways you can show your attitude, too.

Show interest in the children right away. Remember, they're probably feeling unsure of you—and maybe even a little frightened.

Be warm. Use their names. A friendly, *"Hi, Ben. Hey, I like your shoes. Are they new?"* works a lot better than, *"Well, uh, Hi, uh."* No one likes to be called *"uh."* And almost everyone feels better when you occasionally use their name—even the dog.

Show the children that you like kids right off the bat and their parents will know it, too.

Another way to show the family your good attitude is by **asking the right questions**—the responsible questions—before the parents leave. Find out everything you need to know to do your job well.

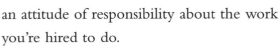

In later chapters, we'll look into what you need to know to do a good job. For now, though, it's enough to say that it's important to have an attitude of responsibility about the work you're hired to do.

When parents see that you've thought about these things, they'll know you're taking your job (and their children) seriously. Your good attitude will shine right through.

Now—**what are the right questions?**

Read on!

Once you've agreed to babysit, you can't change your mind even if your best friend invites you to go someplace you really want to go. But if something happens that means you can't babysit when you've agreed to, call the family as soon as possible. Don't wait to let them know. If you get sick, or if some other emergency occurs and you can't make it, the parents will understand but they will have to get another sitter in a hurry.

CHAPTER 5

WHat DO
THEY EXPECT?

When you buy something, you expect certain things of it. If it's a candy bar, you expect it to taste like candy, not fish food. If it's a sweater, you expect it to keep you warm and not fall apart the first time you wash it.

When parents buy your services as a babysitter, they expect certain things of you. Some parents will tell you their expectations right away, but you may have to ask others a few things.

Start with food. Are

you supposed to feed the kids?
What do they eat and drink? Are
they allowed snacks? What can
they have? Do they eat only in
the kitchen or dining room, or
can they have drinks in the living
room?

Then there's bed-
time. (As you probably know from experience,
children are not always scrupulously honest on this
subject.) What is bedtime for each child? Who gets to
read in bed? Who gets a night-light?

What about baths
before bed? Do any of
the children
need help with
a bath? Are
there smaller
children who need help using the toilet?

No one likes to think about the
whole subject of child abuse. It's a real con-
cern, though, so you do have to think about
it—especially when you are responsible for

children. Make sure there are clear instructions from parents as to how much help and what kind of help their children need in the bathroom or when bathing. This will help set everyone at ease.

Older children may have homework. When and where should they do it? May they stay up until it's done? May they have the TV or music on while they work?

How about chores?
Who puts away the toys? Who clears the table?

Are there pets?
(Are they friendly?) Who feeds them? Walks them?

Are visitors allowed? Can Jenny's friend Jessie visit? Is it okay if Jason from next door comes over to play? Older children may

be allowed to talk with their friends on the phone; if so, who and for how long?

We'll talk about **discipline** in general later, but try to find out special family rules right away. If everyone else knows that when Molly doesn't eat her stewed prunes she doesn't get any brownie delight, then you need to know that, too. If Andrew is sent to his room for a time-out every time he throws a tantrum, you'll want to handle him the same way.

Sometimes there will be **special instructions about medicines**. Never give a child any sort of medicine without full parental knowledge and approval. If medicines are to be given, have a parent write down the schedule and dosage information. The parent should sign the instructions after you've read them aloud to make sure you've gotten it right. As a matter of fact, it's probably a good idea to have a parent write down all important instructions.

It's also a good idea to check out the family's **religious customs** before the parents leave. Do the children say grace before meals? Do they have bedtime prayers? Would they like you to listen to them say their prayers? If so, add a prayer of your own, asking God to bless the children and give them a good night's sleep.

Do the parents expect phone calls or deliveries? Find out what to do if Mr. So-and-So calls or if Mrs. This-or-That drops off the thing that was ordered. Be sure you clearly understand each instruction.

After you've sat for a particular family several times, the parents' expectations will become second nature to you. Until then, don't be afraid to ask questions. No one will think you're silly. In fact, they'll probably consider you one smart sitter!

The forms at the end of this book might help you keep track of the expectations of the families you work for. There is also a form to help you with emergencies. Feel free to alter any of the forms to suit your situation. Keep them together in a place where you can get them when you need them. Parents might appreciate having copies of the forms, too.

One more thing. Parents will want to know how things went. They'll probably ask if the kids were well behaved and if there were any problems. You can let them know all this and more by using the form called **"Sitter's Report"** at the back of this book.

CHAPTER 6

WHat Can YOU EXPect?

The parents who hired you to baby-sit aren't the only people with expectations. You are entitled to some, too, and it's just as important for you to make them clear from the very beginning.

Let's start with the issue of pay. Babysitting rates vary a great deal from community to community. So does the way the rates are figured. Some sitters simply charge a flat rate by the hour. Others charge more for the hours after midnight or for a special occasion, such as during the late Christmas Eve service. Still others charge additional amounts for more than one child. Find out what the going rates and

practices are among your friends. Then let your employers know what you expect. Being a Christian doesn't mean you have to be wishy-washy about pay. **"OH, WeLL, er, anytHing's okay"** is not a good billing practice for anyone. In fact, it can result in confused parents and (sometimes) a resentful you. **"I WOrKeD Here aLL Day for five DOLLars?"**

Money, though, is just one of your expectations. You certainly can expect the parents to tell you every-thing you need to know—including where they are going, how they can be reached while they're gone, and what time they'll be back. Sometimes, of course, people go places where they can't easily be reached, such as to a shopping mall or a concert. But even then you can expect them to give you the number of someone who can act in their place in case of emer-gency. This is a good idea even if they give you a cell phone number. Let's face it. Sometimes cell phones are out of range or drop calls unexpectedly.

You can also expect parents to come home right around the time they've said they will. Anyone can be delayed for a few minutes. But people who habitually drive in an hour or more late are taking advantage of you. That's wrong. Scratch them off your list of employers and let them find other sitters in the future.

If parents have been to a party where alcohol was served, at least one of them should have abstained so

he or she could do the driving—including taking you home. **Never ride home with someone you think has been drinking!** If necessary, call your own parents and ask them to come get you. Refusing to ride with someone who is drunk isn't rude. It's common sense. If the parents who hired you end up embarrassed—tough! Maybe **they'll** be more responsible next time.

You can expect the parents who hire you to provide transportation. If you're going next door, then

maybe it's okay to walk home by yourself at midnight when they return. If the family lives across town, then the issue of getting to their home and then back to yours is a different matter. Don't be shy about asking questions about transportation before you agree to accept the job.

When you take a babysitting job, it is fair for you to expect that your main job will be babysitting. Of course you'll do your best to cope with the orange juice Jacob spilled on the cat. Of course you'll clear the supper dishes if you've fed the children. But no one should expect you to do yesterday's breakfast dishes or the laundry that just happens to have piled up in the basement or to run the vacuum cleaner over the living room carpet or even just dust around the edges a little. There aren't many people who would even ask such things of you. But if you run into someone who does, remember that you have the right to say no (politely), and, if necessary, to scratch them off your list.

You may actually find times when you **want** to do something special, when parents you've grown to like a lot have had to dash off and leave the house a mess. Then the urge to do some cleaning up may be more than you can resist. You're doing it as a gift of love. That's different.

And last, you should expect to be in a safe environment. If you feel uneasy about something or threatened in any way, be brave and mature, but be alert, too. Remember, you can always call the parents at the phone number they've given you. And you can always call your own parents if you have concerns.

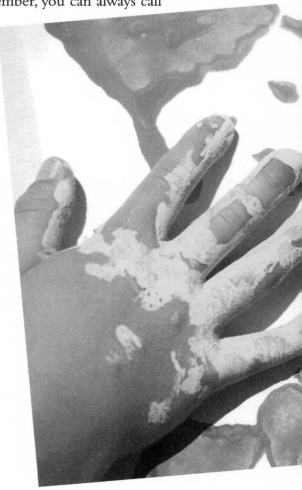

CHAPTER 7

THE PERQS

Perqs. That's business slang for perquisites, the extra benefits that come with a job. Babysitters get their share of perqs, too, and these can vary from place to place. It's always best to know what the parents are giving before you do any taking.

One perq you'll sometimes be offered is free food. Some parents will even go so far as to say, "Eat anything in the refrigerator that looks good to you." Then your common sense must prevail. Maybe you **can** wolf down an entire chocolate cream pie. But will your body get even with you later? And what will even the most generous of parents secretly think about you? Other parents will be more specific, "If you get hungry, there are potato chips, fruit juice, and carrot sticks." In that case, keep your grubby paws away from the pie.

A few folks may actually forget that people your age like to munch a lot. Grin and bear the hunger pangs the first time this happens. But the next time you work there, tuck a goody from home into your pocket or backpack. Just don't eat it in front of the children. **That's mean!**

A humongous TV with 934 fascinating channels, a complete library of DVDs and video games, or some other electronic marvel may also be among the perqs you're offered. Just be sure you understand the rules governing your use of them. No fair switching off "Sesame Street" so you can watch "The Bionic Octopus."

What about having friends over while you're sitting—you know, just to keep you company? Frankly, most parents don't like that idea. They've hired you to care for their children, and that's what they want you to do. But if some parents say it's okay for you to have someone over, be sure not to abuse the privilege and invite your whole group of friends.

Telephone privileges are another area where you'll want to be careful. Sometimes you just **have** to call someone to find out your math assignment or see if you got a part in the play. Always keep such calls short, though. You never know. The parents might be trying to call **you**—and 30 minutes of straight busy signal could make them downright crabby.

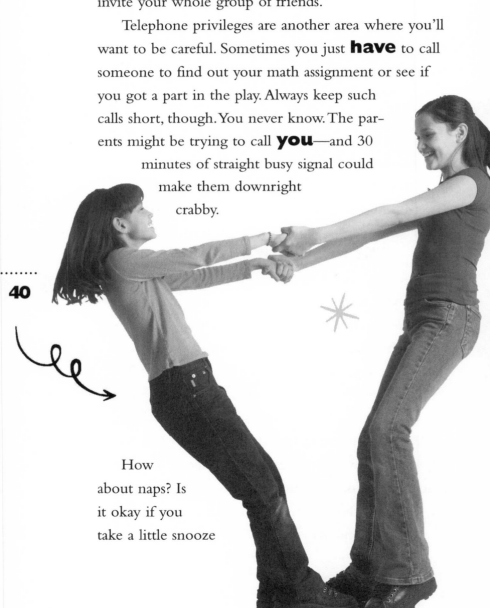

How about naps? Is it okay if you take a little snooze

after the kids are in bed? Some parents say, "Fine," especially if they plan to be out late. Others would rather you didn't. They're afraid something might go wrong—such as a child getting sick—and you might not wake up. Find out how the parents you're working for feel about sleeping on the job. Then respect their wishes. But if you are a really heavy sleeper, it might not be a good idea to snooze.

One of the best things about sitting is that sometimes you can do two things at once—such as sit and study. That's great. But there will also be times when you can't study, when the children will demand every ounce of your attention and energy. At those times the books simply have to go.

You must never—**ever**—put any of the perqs before your job, which is taking care of the children. If you really need to study or spend a Saturday night with your friends or catch up on your sleep, figure that out ahead of time and don't take the babysitting job.

Part of servanthood is stewardship, and stewardship isn't just putting a percentage of your earnings into the collection plate each Sunday. It's also using your time, talents, and energy in the best possible way—for others and for you.

CHAPTER 8

TECHNOLOGY ON THE JOB

So you're a techno-junkie who breaks into a cold sweat after an hour away from your cell phone and Internet connection. Is it okay to sneak in a little text messaging with your friends while you're sitting? Or maybe you are babysitting kids whose parents are apparently techno-junkies, too. When you walk into the house, you practically have to wipe the drool off your chin. You are surrounded by the equipment of your dreams. Is it okay to use it?

Well, it's probably not a good idea to bring along a lot of electronic equipment from home. Certainly leave behind anything requiring headphones. It is inconsiderate to the kids to use them when they are awake. It can even keep you from hearing a cry when they are supposed to be asleep. If you are looking to bring something to do after bedtime, a book or magazine might be a better choice.

From a safety perspective, however, if you have a cell phone, it's probably a good idea to bring it on the job. It means you have a help line at your fingertips at all times. It also means you have a phone available whenever you need it, even if the power goes out. And using your own cell phone means you aren't tying up the family's phone should the parents call to check on things. This is **not**, however, the time to have a lengthy chat with your friend, especially if the kids are awake. A quick call to check on an assignment is probably okay. Just keep it short. And never make long-distance phone calls unless it's an emergency.

Once again, the thing to remember is that taking care of the kids is your job. Don't let your techno-cravings, or anything else for that matter, interfere with it.

So what about their stuff? Is it okay to use all that great equipment? A good rule of thumb is to always ask first. If you think about it, wouldn't you want someone to ask before messing with **your** cool stuff? (Remember that you are a guest in their home!) If you get a no or a hesitant yes in reply—or if you don't ask—then you'd better leave it alone.

It's also a good idea to ask whether the kids can use the equip- ment. Let's face it. They may be better than you are at getting the stuff to work, but they may also be waiting for a chance to get **their** hands on their parents' cool stuff when they're not around. If you're not sure who is allowed to touch what stuff, it's best to do something else instead.

Another thing to ask parents is what media the

kids are allowed to consume. Which shows or DVDs are okay to watch? What music is okay to listen to? What video games may be played? Can the kids use the computer? The VCR? What about the phone? What kinds of time limits are enforced for these things? Be specific!

When it comes to computers and you, a hands-off policy is best. Personal computers are just that—personal. You don't want to end up at a file or site where you don't belong. You also don't want to do anything that might crash a hard drive, delete a file, or invite in a virus. Computers are very useful tools, but they can cost a lot of time and money to repair if something gets messed up.

So, although the tech equipment seems to be calling you, you have to know the house rules concerning its use. Playing games or doing things with the kids that are parent-approved is fine. Just wait to feed your techno-cravings on your own time—with your own equipment. And don't allow yourself to be distracted from your responsibility—caring for the children.

CHAPTER 9

Kids Are People Too

Parents are an important part of your career as a babysitter. So, obviously, are you. But most important of all are the children. Face it, without them you'd be out of a job. Not many folks hire someone to sit with their fish.

But people—even people your age—tend to forget fast what it's like to be a kid. Some folks look down on them. They think they're just insignificant little savages who haven't grown up yet or inferior beings that are fun to order around.

These folks are wrong. Children are God's creatures, just like you and everyone else. God's Son died and rose for them, just as He did for everyone else. It is wrong to think of them as insignificant or inferior. Of course other folks get so mushily carried away by how cute children can be that they expect them to behave like angels all the time. They're wrong, too.

Children are sinners—just like you and me and anyone else. Dainty little Danielle may well bop the baby over the head with her doll.

Curly-haired Curtis may bite you on the knee. Kids are people. They have feelings. Some of those feelings are good. Some aren't. It's up to you to bring out as many of the good feelings as you can. If you act like a drill sergeant and boss kids around all the time, they're likely to burst—usually into tears or tantrums. Those aren't the kinds of feelings you want to bring out. On the other hand, if you approach kids with all the backbone of a wet dishrag, they may try to take over. They'll defy you—or sneak around you. Those aren't the kinds of feelings you want to bring out, either.

We'll get around to the matter of discipline later. For now, it's good to remember that kids tend to give you what you expect them to give you. Expect them to be brats and they probably won't disappoint you. Expect them to be normal, healthy, and sometimes even helpful little human beings, and that's probably what you'll get.

Speaking of helpful, sometimes kids—especially little ones—will just beg to help you clear the table, clean up the puddle, whatever. (As soon as they're old enough to be of any real help, most kids lose this impulse.) You know you could do the job better and in much less time by yourself. Well, forget time. Forget quality. Generations of mothers have made the sacrifice of letting their children help them because it means so much to the helpers. Swallow your impatience and join their club.

Kids are people. Like other people, they're all different. You have to get to know them one at a time before you can have a really good relationship with them.

Shy Suzanne may need to sit in the corner with her teddy bear for half an hour before she'll warm up to you. She'll probably burst into tears if you look at her cross-eyed. When Suzanne does something wrong, a gentle **"THat's not a good idea"** is usually enough to stop her.

Bubba, on the other hand, charges at you like a tractor trailer the minute you arrive. The faces he can make are enough to leave *you* in tears. You may have to be very firm just to get his attention when he does something wrong.

But different as they are, Suzanne and Bubba are both equally precious to God. As you get to know them and try to understand them, they'll probably end up equally precious to you, too.

Kids are people. As with other people, sometimes you'll have good times with them and sometimes you'll have bad. Sometimes you'll end up flat on your back on the floor with all of them on top of you. There, at the bottom of that giggling heap, you'll thank God for such moments. Other times you'll end up collapsed on the couch, your nerves in shreds after an evening of screams, disobedience, and back talk. Talk to God then, too. Ask Him to help you remember to forgive. And thank Him for forgiving you through Jesus.

You see, kids are people—God's own creation. You can't remind yourself of that too often. The best way to deal with them is the way God deals with all His people. Love—and forgive—them because of the love He gives to us.

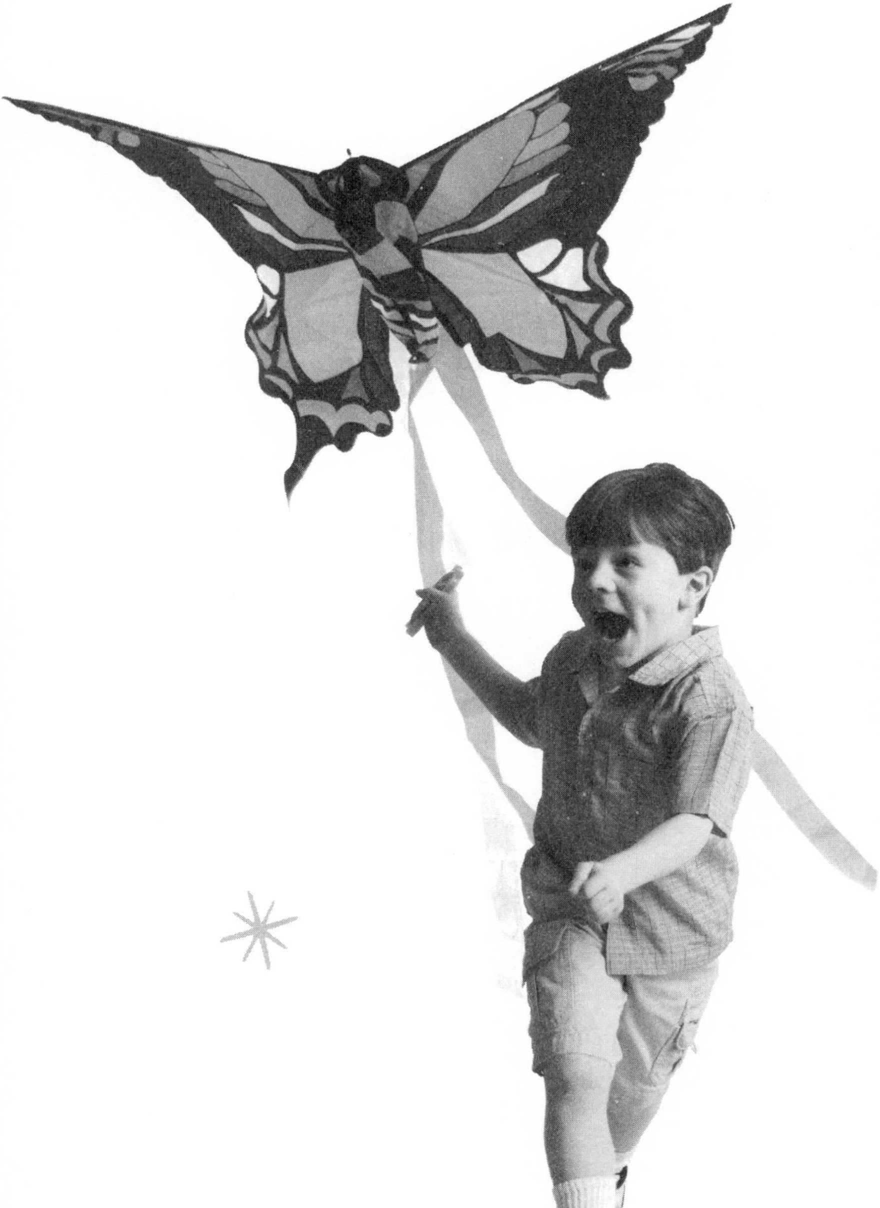

CHAPTER 10

Your Toolbox

Would Mighty Mortal leap into the air without his magic cape? Would Chef Yummier go near a kitchen without salt and pepper? Would Dr. Snipandsew rush to a patient's aid without his little black bag? Of course not. Most professionals wouldn't be caught without the tools of their trade. But many babysitters come to the job with nothing more than their bare hands. That's because they often don't realize that their trade has tools. It does. You, too, can show up for work complete with a toolbox.

Okay—maybe it isn't a real toolbox. But wise sitters prepare their own bag to take with them on jobs. It can be anything from a backpack to a tote to a plain brown paper sack. Some sitters decorate their bags specially to appeal to kids. Paint or crayon on brown paper looks cheerful (although the paper may not hold up for more than one night). Felt glued to a canvas or cloth tote (or shapes cut from iron-on patches) is more durable. You can use fabric paint on canvas too.

No matter how your bag looks, though, it's what's inside that is important. This might include coloring books, crayons, storybooks, appropriate videos or DVDs, puzzles, toy cars, games, a stuffed toy, or anything else you think the children might enjoy. There's no reason why some of these things can't be religious, either. Christian bookstores are crammed with items especially for children. Your job gives you the opportunity to help children learn about Jesus while you play.

"But all the kids I sit for have plenty of toys of their own," you might say. Ah, yes, but those are old, familiar toys. Children are always fascinated by something different, something that belongs to someone else. Remember how you used to feel

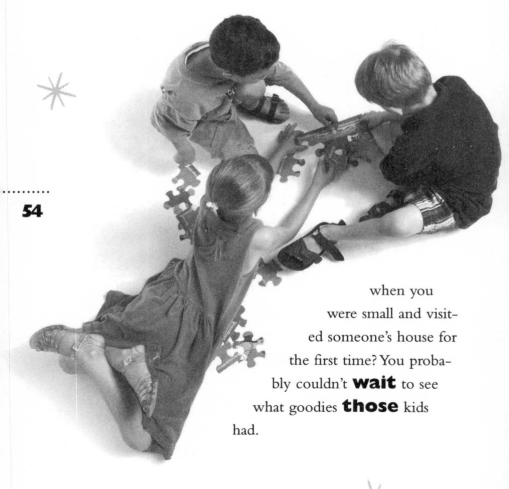

when you were small and visited someone's house for the first time? You probably couldn't **wait** to see what goodies **those** kids had.

You don't have to spend a lot on your bag of tricks, either. Sometimes stuff left over from your own childhood will do very well. Toys needn't be **new** to appeal to children—just different. Besides, you can always take materials to make things—such as puppets. Lunch-size paper bags can be trimmed and decorated into really cute biblical characters. Draw on faces. Curl construction paper for hair and beards or use cotton for older characters. Paste on fabric or gift wrap for robes. Then add any other finishing touches that seem a good idea to you at the time. You can use puppets such as these to tell the children Bible stories. Or let the kids act out the stories with you. Older children might enjoy making puppets of their own.

You can easily make another sort of puppet from a pair of old socks and a few scraps. First, stuff one sock into the toe of the other. Place your hand in the outer sock, with your fingers extending into the toe (above the inner sock), and your thumb extending downward into the heel. You've now formed the puppet's head and lower jaw. Sew on two matching buttons for eyes and a different button for a nose. Make a hat, tie, tongue, or whatever you like from scraps of felt or other cloth. Yarn hair or a fancy bow can transform your puppet into a girl. **Presto!** What do you end up with? Who knows? It can be a dragon, a sea serpent, a worm, a dinosaur, or whatever you want it to be. Then just give it a name and introduce it to the children.

Don't worry about not being a professional ventriloquist, either. Hold the puppet some distance from your face and make your voice higher or lower when you speak for it. No one will notice—or care—that your lips are moving or that the voice is coming from you. Before you know it, the kids will accept Snuffers (or whomever) as a real person. Sometimes they'll even tell it things they wouldn't dream of saying to you! Sometimes they may **listen** to it when they don't want to listen to you!

The simplest materials often turn out to be the best toys of all.

A blank pad of paper can provide hours of enjoyment for kids. Do you know how to fold paper into a hat or a boat? Do it for the kids. Then show them how. Have you ever folded and cut paper to make snowflakes or doilies or Christmas trees or a line of paper dolls? What's old stuff to you may be a brand-new game for the children you're watching.

Can you draw—at all? Kids love to have older people teach them to draw even the sim-

plest things. You can even use simple figures to illus-
trate a Bible story.

Children also enjoy drawing stained glass windows—and they're simple. Have them start by using a
pencil to make a big squiggly design on a piece of
paper. Then have them color in the spaces with
crayons or markers. Finally, have them go over the
pencil lines with black crayon or marker. It's a stained-
glass window! Now all you have to do is get an old
cardboard box and make a church. . .

"Me-dolls" are fun, too. If you can get huge sheets or a roll of blank paper, great, otherwise you can tape together regular newsprint pages. Have the child lie down on the paper and draw around him or her. Cut out the shape and have the child fill in face, hair, clothes, etc.

Then there's string. Do you know how to make a cat's cradle—or any of those other mysterious string creations? Do it for the kids. They'll beg you for encore after encore.

What else do you remember liking to do when you were younger? Chances are your small charges will like it just as much.

Many sitters have found one other item very useful in their bag of tricks—**a notebook**. In it they keep a special section for each child. This section includes name, age, likes and dislikes, favorite stories, favorite prayers, neat things that have happened in the past, etc. A quick review of these pages can help you stay right on top of the situation when you return to a home where you haven't been for a while—especially if you do a lot of sitting for a lot of different families. Your sitter's notebook is also a good place to keep that checklist of questions to ask each new family, as well as the pages of emergency numbers we'll talk about later. The back of this book has a section that can help you get started on your own notebook.

Good grief! This sure means an awful lot of work! Is that what you're thinking by now? Well, in a way you're right. You may spend a few hours putting together your bag of tricks and notebook. And you probably won't earn any more money with them than you would have without. But you will earn more in other ways. Sooner or later, you'll begin to see the kids' eyes light up when they see you coming. You just might have as much fun with the puppets and other projects as they do. You'll know that old-fashioned (but still wonderful) feeling of a job well done. Above all, you'll know you've given your best to a service you are doing for God.

CHAPTER 11

playtime

In a way, it's another of the perqs of babysitting. You get **paid** to play. True, the games might not be those you'd choose to play with your friends, but that doesn't mean they can't be fun (especially if you can forget for a while how old and dignified you are).

Some sitters think they can get by with plopping on the couch and telling the kids to go play by themselves. There might be times when children really do prefer to play alone, but usually kids love to have you join in their games. It makes everything so much more fun. (You remember, don't you?) And when the kids are having more fun, you're doing a better job, which is what you want, isn't it?

Playtime can also give you a chance to do some religious education with your charges—painlessly. As long as you know the family is Christian, you don't have to worry too much about crossing denominational lines. Most children's games (including those that follow) work just as well for little Lutherans, Methodists, Roman Catholics, or whatevers. Here are some suggestions. You can probably add more ideas of your own.

Baby Games

Peek-a-boo

Sure, you know that one. You cover your face with your hands and say *"All gone!"* Then move your hands away and say *"peek-a-boo!"* Baby shrieks with delight.

So make just one addition. When you move your hands away, say *"peek-a-boo! God loves you!"* Will baby understand? Maybe. Maybe not. You never know.

Patacake

That's an old favorite, too. With just a few changes, you have:

Patacake, patacake, God's own child.
(Clap child's hands together.)

Mix up a cake all fluffy and wild.
(Make stirring motions with child's hands.)

Roll it and toss it and give it a prod.
(Perform these actions with child's hands.)

Then bake it and give your thanks to God.
(Place palms of child's hands together.)

Here's a Foreheadthumper

This is an old German game (and it sounds very impressive indeed in German). Touch the child in the corresponding place as you name each body part. As you say the last line, gently tickle the child.

Here's a foreheadthumper,
And here's an eyeblinker,
And here's a noseschnuffler,
And here's a mouthgrinner,
And here's a chinchinner,
A-n-n-n-d God made them all!

Action poems

Preschoolers get a real charge out of these. See if you can come up with some of your own.

The Good Samaritan

A man on a highway a long time ago
Was taking a trip down to old Jericho.
(Make walking motions with fingers.)

Some robbers attacked him and left him half dead,
His body all aching, a bump on his head.
(Rub head and moan.)

Along came a priest, and he passed right on by.
"I can't stop to help him. Oh no, no! Not I!"
(Shake head vigorously.)

Now next came a Levite, and he passed by too.
"I simply can't stop! I have too much to do!"
(Shake head again.)

At last a Samaritan came riding by.
He bandaged the poor man so he wouldn't die.
(Pretend to wind bandages.)

Then on his own donkey, took him to an inn
And paid for his care till he felt well again.
(Wave arms and stamp feet.)

Jesus and the Storm

A little wooden boat was floating on the deep.
(Make wavelike motions with hands.)

Jesus' friends were talking. Jesus was asleep.
(Pretend to be asleep.)

Then rain began to fall. First came the little drops.
(Wiggle fingers and move hands downward.)

Then the middle-sized ones.
Last came the great big plops.
(Cover head.)

The wind began to blow.
It blew and blew and blew.
(Make wind noises.)

The waves began to grow.
They grew and grew and grew.
(Raise hands above head.)

Now Jesus' friends were scared.
They thought their boat would tip.
(Lean way to one side.)

They started calling out,
"Please, Lord, save our ship!"
(Cup hands at mouth as if calling.)

So Jesus stopped the wind.
He made the waves get small.
(Raise hands above head, then lower them.)

And to His friends He said,
"I'll take care of you all."
(Spread arms wide.)

The 10 Men

In Jesus' day there lived 10 men.
They all were very sick.
(Hold up 10 fingers.)

"Jesus, You're our Friend!" they cried.
"Help us get well quick."
(Hold out hands as if pleading.)

So Jesus made them well again,
And nine men ran away.
(Make running motions with fingers.)

Just one told Jesus, "Thank You, Lord!"
He shared God's love, I'd say.
(Hold up one finger.)

Motion Games

Although it may seem as though some kids prefer to sit glued to a television set for hours, the time does come when they simply **have** to move around. When the children you're babysitting have reached their limit (or their parents' limit), try some of these games.

Mother, May I?

It's the old game with a new twist. One person is the leader and tells the others to perform various actions. In this case, though, make them religious actions.

"Caitlin, bow your head."
"Sam, sing a hymn."
"Sabrina, kneel down."

Of course the person is supposed to say, "Mother, may I?" before performing the action. Whoever forgets is out of the game. The last person remaining gets to be leader in the next game.

Here We Go 'Round the Mulberry Bush

Another old favorite, but instead of acting out the usual verses ("This is the way we wash the clothes," etc.), try some of these:

"This is the way we go to church,
Go to church, go to church.
This is the way we go to church
So early in the morning."

"This is the way we say a prayer. . ."

"This is the way we sing to God. . ."

"This is the way we hear God's Word. . ."

Can you think of more verses?

Bible Story Charades

You probably won't play this one with two teams as you usually do, unless you're sitting for a *lot* of kids. But one person can think of a Bible story and act it out for the others to guess.

Quiet Games

When you think you can't possibly move another muscle, it's time to switch to some quiet games. Here are a couple:

I'm Thinking of Something

Everyone sits. Then you look around the room, choose an object, and say, "I'm thinking of something in God's world, and it's (blue or funny or huge or whatever)." The other players take turns guessing what you're thinking of. Whoever guesses right gets to be the next thinker.

Add-on Story

The rules for this game are simple, too. You make up the beginning of the story.

"Once upon a time, there was a little boy who was afraid of milk shakes. Milk shakes scared him silly. One day he had to go to the ice cream parlor with his mother. There on the counter stood a huge milk shake. The little boy took one look at it and. . . ."

Stop and let one of the children continue the story. After he or she has carried on the action for a while, let another child take over. You can go on taking turns in this game until you're all out of ideas—or giggling so hard that you can't talk.

Now that you've got a few games to start you off, do some thinking of your own. What games do **you** remember from **your** childhood?

Playtime

CHAPTER 12

Story Time

"Tell me a story!"

It's one of the most ancient chants of childhood. Kids will promise almost anything for a story—to brush their teeth, to go to bed, maybe even to eat their broccoli.

Story time is also a good way to quiet kids down after a bout of rough-and-tumble, or to put them in the mood for bed. Something about a voice spinning on and on makes the pillow seem less like the enemy.

If you enjoy making up and telling your own tales, by all means do it. Kids are immensely flattered by original, just-for-us stories. But they won't be disappointed if you read or tell them other people's stories. When you stop to think about it, the best and most exciting stories in the world are in the Bible.

Whether you're reading or telling a tale, there are a few simple tricks that can make it more fun for the kids—and for you. Try using different voices for different characters. Make them **very** different—super high, rumbly low, slo-o-ow as molasses, or super quick. You can also use your voice to build suspense. Make it softer and more intense at scary moments. Then, when the action gets hot and hairy, let yourself go! Insert sound effects at appropriate points in the story.

"THen tHe tHUnDer crasHeD.

RUMBLE-BOOM! THE Lightning flashed. Ziggety-Zizzety-JAG! THE waves beat against the little boat. SLOSH! SLOSH! Boy, were Jesus' friends scared then!" Fun, isn't it?

Be sure to let the kids see all the pictures when you're reading from a book. Small children like to stop right in the middle of a story and talk about what they see.

"WHat's tHat, CHristoPHer?"

"An eLePHant."

"AnD WHO'S tHat beHinD tHe busH?"

"ADam."

Sooner or later, some child is going to ask you a question that makes your toes curl.

"WHere DiD NoaH Put aLL tHe animals?"

"WHY DiDn't Jesus kill tHe baD guys?"

Think carefully before you answer. Don't be afraid to admit it when you don't know something. Tell the kids you'll find out—maybe from your pastor—and let them know the next time you come. (Just don't forget to do it.)

Do you remember playing dress-up in cast-off grown-up clothes when you were little? Fun, huh? If you never did, now's the time to start. See what old stuff—hats, belts, funny gloves—you can find around your house and drag it along with you. (You may want to wait until at least the second time you sit for a family.) Then choose a Bible story, assign the roles to the kids, and use what you have as costumes. Someone should read the story aloud first, so everyone has the facts straight. Then let yourselves go and act it out.

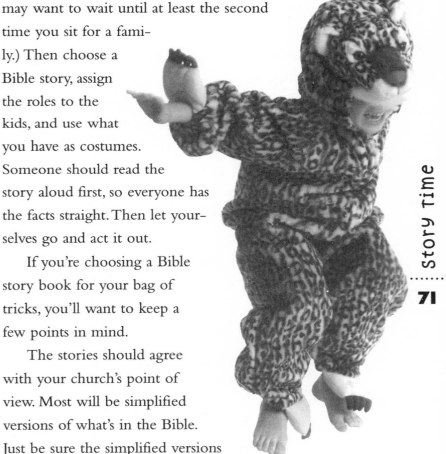

If you're choosing a Bible story book for your bag of tricks, you'll want to keep a few points in mind.

The stories should agree with your church's point of view. Most will be simplified versions of what's in the Bible. Just be sure the simplified versions don't wander away from the truth.

The pictures should be bright, colorful, and true. True pictures? Well, remember that Jesus lived in the Middle East. We don't know exactly what He looked like. But we can be pretty sure He didn't have blond hair and blue eyes.

The book should be sturdy and well made. You don't want one of your charges to eat it when you're not looking.

Check your shelves or boxes for books you liked when you were young and bring a few along. Make sure the books you choose match the ages of the kids you're sitting. And try to bring a few different books—picture books, prayer books, even a devotional to read at bedtime. The kids will be enthused about whatever you bring and will probably listen closely to whatever you read. This is a great way to share Jesus' love with someone else and to share your faith in Him as our Savior. Like everything else you do when you babysit—it's serving God.

If you don't have a big collection of books at home, your local Christian bookstore will have plenty to choose from. In fact, there are so many books available you'll have trouble choosing. The following list of books from Concordia Publishing House might help get you started.

- **THE Little Visits** series of devotionals
- **THE Very First Christmas,**

  THE Very First Easter, and

  THE Very First Christians by Paul L. Maier
- **THE Kids Bible** by Leana Lane
- **My First Bible** by Leena Lane
- **THE Story of Jesus** by Christopher Doyle
- **One Hundred Bible Stories**
- **A Child's Garden of Bible Stories**
- **Toddler's Action Bible** by Robin Currie
- **My Bible Story Book** by Sarah Fletcher
- **3 in 1: A Picture of God** by Joanne Marxhausen
- **Heaven Is a Wonderful Place** by Joanne Marxhausen

Story time

73

CHAPTER 13

THE SOUND of MUSIC

What kind of music do you like? Chances are the kids you're watching will like it, too.

They haven't had much chance to form their own musical tastes yet, so they'll probably enjoy "Blizzard" by The Fat Turtle as well as Vivaldi's "The Four Seasons." (Be sure to get permission from parents before playing music for their children and for using sound equipment in the homes you're visiting.)

What children enjoy most of all is making music themselves. It's a great way to entertain them—and you—while you're sitting. Of course, if you can accompany the songs you sing on piano, guitar, ukulele, kazoo, or whatever, all the better. But a little enthusiastic warbling on your part (with the emphasis on enthusiastic) is really all it takes to get the kids going.

You might consider making some rhythm instruments to carry along in your bag of tricks. Oatmeal cartons or coffee cans covered with gift-wrap make good drums. Use unsharpened pencils for drumsticks. Other small containers with plastic lids make delightfully noisy shakers when you put unpopped corn, dried beans, beads, or pebbles in them. Sew a few jingle bells to an elastic wristband to give you all the Christmas spirit—even in July.

Small children love to make up actions to go with the songs they're singing. The songs that follow will give you some ideas, but you can easily make up more on your own.

Older children often like to make up new words for songs they already know. For example, to the tune of **"Old MacDonald Had a Farm,"** sing:

> *God made such a pretty world.*
> $E - I - E - I - O$
> *And in that world He put some ducks.*
> $E - I - E - I - O$
> *With a quack-quack here*
>   *and a quack-quack there,*
> *Here a quack, there a quack,*
>   *everywhere a quack-quack.*
> *God made such a pretty world.*
> $E - I - E - I - O$

(Of course the stanzas can go on forever.)

Then there's **"Mary Had a Little Lamb."**

> *Peter had a little boat,*
> *Little boat, little boat.*
> *Peter had a little boat.*
> *He went to catch some fish.*

Your turn! Try making up some songs with the children. And try learning some of these songs together. If you know songs from Sunday School or Vacation Bible School, you can teach them to the kids too. Almost everyone learns **"Jesus Loves Me."** It's even more meaningful when you sing it together.

CHAPTER 14

prayer time

You'll want to be a little sensitive when it comes to the matter of prayer—especially if the children you're watching are of another faith. But if they go to your church, you can be pretty sure the prayers you like will be fine for them too.

If the children already say regular bedtime prayers and mealtime graces, by all means let them use them. But you can also teach them new ones (to surprise Mom and Dad).

Use the prayers you remember from your childhood. Or, try some of these:

Loving Jesus, gentle Lamb,
In Thy gracious hands I am.
Make me, Savior, what Thou art.
Live Thyself within my heart.

(Charles Wesley)

Father in heaven,
be with all the people
who take care of me—
my mommy and daddy,
my brothers and sisters,
my grandma and grandpa,
my aunts and uncles and cousins,
and my babysitters.
I'm glad they love me.

(Lois Walfrid Johnson)

Teach me, my God and King,
In all things Thee to see,
That what I do in anything,
To do it as for Thee.

(George Herbert)

All good gifts around us
Are sent from heaven above.
Then thank the Lord,
Oh, thank the Lord,
For all His love.

(Jane Montgomery Campbell)

Thank You for the food we eat.
Let children everywhere
Have just as much to thank You for.
Please, God, hear our prayer.

(Sarah Fletcher)

Be near me, Lord Jesus; I ask You to stay
Close by me forever and love me, I pray.
Bless all the dear children in Your tender care
And fit us for heaven to live with You there.

(Cradle Song)

You might also want to look at the following books from Concordia Publishing House:

- **Prayers for Little People** by Sarah Fletcher

- **God's Children Pray** by Mary Manz Simon

- **A Child's Garden of Prayer**

- **Little Folded Hands** by Allan Hart Jahsmann

- **Prayer** by Jeanette L. Groth

- **Psalms for Kids** by Robert Baden

CHAPTER 15

Discipline. . .

Or, How to Get Kids to Do What THey Don't Want to Do or Stop Doing What THey Want to Do

Sounds like a tall order, doesn't it? Well, don't start nibbling your nails just yet. A few hints should help you trim it down to size.

Did you ever notice that the words *discipline* and *disciple* are a lot alike? And *disciple* means "follower." H – m – m – m. If you could just get the kids to **follow** your wishes because they want to, your discipline problems would be solved. But how can you do that?

Let's start with a few dos and don'ts.

Do forgive. Remind yourself of your own mistakes and of all the times someone else forgave you. Then think about God's forgiveness. He sent Jesus to suffer and die for the world's sin—Jesus took the punishment for our sin in our place. That's why we can forgive others—because God forgives us first.

And say it aloud. Sometimes saying **"I forgive you"** has more impact than any other sentence.

Don't be an ogre. There's something about hearing orders barked at them that makes a lot of people—including kids—just **have** to rebel. Don't set yourself and the kids up like that. Besides, no one loves an ogre.

Don't be wishy-washy. **"O-H-H-H, I DON't KNOW. MAYBE YOU SORT OF OUGHtN't tO DO tHAt—HUH?"** Faced with that limp-noodle attitude, any red-blooded kid is going to get by with all he or she can.

Do refer to parents' guidelines. If Mom and Dad said no TV after 9:00, let the kids know you consider that rule carved in stone. Most likely they'll agree with you, especially since Mom and Dad aren't around to be whined at.

Don't lose your cool. The minute you burst into tears—or fall on the floor and scream and kick your feet—the kids have gained control. Your job is to be on top of the situation—always, even if you suspect you're going mad.

Don't go to extremes. Sitting Charlie in the corner for two hours is too much. And never, **ever** use physical punishment, such as hitting, shaking, or spanking a child. Your ultimate threat should be, "If you don't do that (or stop doing that), I'm going to have to tell your parents." Use this threat sparingly. But if you do use it, follow through.

Do try humor sometimes. It's one of God's greatest gifts to us. Sometimes a mock-serious statement such as "If you don't brush your teeth right now, I'm going to put you in the encyclopedia" does wonders. Especially if you follow it up with a firm "March!"

Don't be sarcastic with the kids or put them down. You may win temporarily, but it's a cheap victory. Sarcasm and other hurtful words open wounds and destroy the child's trust in you. You don't want to do that.

Sometimes you can almost feel the shift of control happen. One minute the struggle is still on—the struggle to determine who's in charge. The next minute you say or do something right and—presto! You're the boss.

In the long run, you'll find that you have the fewest discipline problems with the kids who like you best—the kids who respect you and really want your approval. And that's not so unusual. Isn't that how **you** react to the people responsible for you? Take another look at chapter 9. Kids are people.

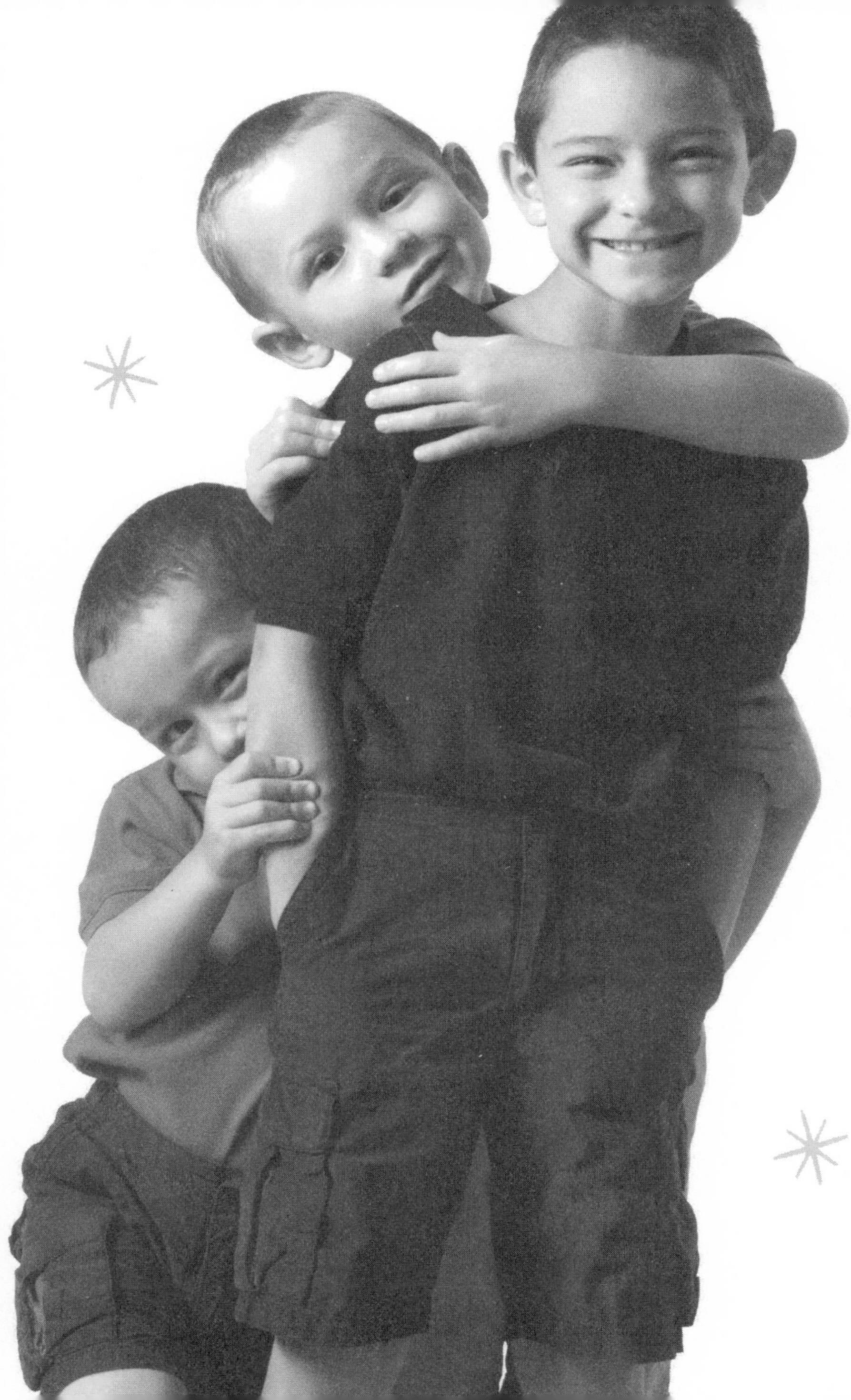

CHAPTER 16

Emergency!

Okay, they do happen sometimes—honest-to-goodness emergencies. And you're in charge. You have to deal.

Sure, that's a scary thought. But a little thinking ahead, a little planning for what you would do **if**, can make all the difference. It can mean you won't panic. It can mean you'll make the best possible decisions. It can mean, sometimes, the difference between life and death.

Of course you would follow the same safety rules and emergency procedures you have at home. But let's think ahead a bit. What would you do in an emergency while you're babysitting?

First, you'd want to make sure it's a real emergency. Suppose two kids are fighting over which TV program to watch. That's no emergency. If you call Mr. and Mrs. Jones away from their gourmet dinner at a romantic restaurant to solve that sort of problem, you aren't much of a sitter.

But what if you suddenly have to cope with a seriously ill or hurt child, a fire, or a suspected prowler outside? Those are emergencies.

Say a prayer. It needn't be fancy. **"Lord, Help me"** will do. Of course, He **will** help you—whether you ask or not. But saying that prayer helps **you** remember that He's there with you.

Stay calm. Even if your insides are quivering like Jell-O, wear a cool, competent mask on the outside. You owe that to the children in your care. And it'll probably help you feel calmer too. (One trick that sometimes works is to pretend that you're your own mother or father and act the way you think she or he would in this situation.)

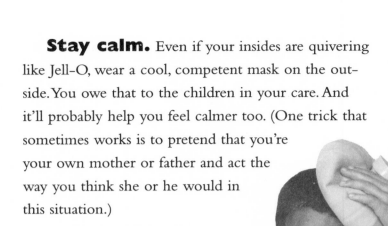

Get human help.

No one expects you to handle a serious emergency alone. Remember those phone numbers the parents gave you? Use them. Almost all areas have an all-purpose emergency number—911—to call for fire, police, ambulance, etc. If you do not live in a 911 call area, be sure you know the emergency phone number.

At the end of this chapter, you'll find a page on which to write all sorts of important information and emergency phone numbers. Make enough copies of it so you have one for every family for which you sit.

Ask parents to fill out the sheet the first time you work for them. Then keep it in your sitter's notebook or carry it with you each time you go to that home.

Use common sense. Sometimes things happen that you can't plan for. Suppose a candle suddenly explodes and flames begin creeping up the wall. That really did happen to one sitter. The parents had lit a candle in their dining room and then had forgotten about it. The first the sitter knew that there was trouble was when the six-year-old yelled, "THe Dining room's on fire!" It was a freezing-cold winter night. But the sitter's common sense told her that fire was far more dangerous than cold. So, without waiting to put on coats, she got herself and the child out of that house and to a neighbor's. From there she dialed 911. The fire engines arrived in time to prevent any major damage. And two grateful parents couldn't stop praising the sitter for her quick and sound thinking.

Here are a few more hints to help you handle—or avoid—emergency situations.

- **Know where** all the phones are in the house so you can call from the nearest one, if necessary.

- **Know how** to operate the locks on the doors. This is especially important if a house has deadbolt locks that must be opened with a key from the inside too. Be sure you know exactly where those keys are.

- **Keep all** doors and windows locked. Don't let in anyone except the children's parents or your own.

- **Keep dangerous** items (knives, medicines, matches, cleansers, etc.) out of the children's reach. Make sure handles of pots and skillets that are on the stove are turned so they are out of reach as well.

- **Don't leave** any potential source of fire unwatched. This includes candles and cooking food. In fact, don't light candles at all.

- **Try to** keep small children where you can see them every moment (unless they're asleep). Never leave children unattended or alone in the house.

- **Know where** the family keeps their first-aid kit. Not all emergencies are biggies. You can probably doctor a scraped elbow or knee without calling the paramedics.

- **Know the** escape routes. If you have to leave the house in a hurry, it's important to know the safest door or window to use. In addition to that, know which neighbor is closest and who is at home to offer safe shelter for you and the children you are responsible for.

If you're worried or have a question about something, remember that you can always call **your** parents. After all, they know a lot about taking care of kids. Look what a good job they did with you!

CHAPTER 17

Let's Go!

In this chapter, you'll find some last minute suggestions to help you make sure you're prepared to do the best job possible.

What's here:

- Important things to do in the days (or hours) before you actually go babysit.

- Suggestions for what to include in your Sitter's Toolbox (or Backpack)

- Suggestions for what to include in your Sitter's Notebook

- The forms we talked about earlier. Copy them or adapt them to suit you.

First, though, follow these steps before every babysitting job:

- **Get as** much information about when, where, and who you'll be working for. Get a phone number to call back if you have questions.
- **Leave the** family's name, address, and phone number with your parents. Always make sure someone at home knows where you are and can get in touch with you, even if it means you have to write a note and tape it to the refrigerator.
- **Decide if** you'll take anything with you (see the Sitter's Toolbox list below).

- **Make copies** of the information forms you want to take, or have paper and a list of information you need in a notebook to take with you.
- **Give yourself** plenty of time to get ready. You'll want to be ready and waiting for your babysitting job to start the minute Mr. or Mrs. Parent arrives to pick you up. And wear comfortable clothes—you might be playing hard or even taking a nap.
- **Say a** prayer. Remember that as a babysitter, you serve God in an important ministry. You are taking responsibility for someone else, for a child of God. Ask God to guide you and keep you as you work. And thank Him for the opportunity to serve Him in Jesus' name.

Sitter's Toolbox (or Backpack)

In chapter 10, we talked about things to take with you when you go babysit. Your toolbox can be the item of interest—the curiosity bag—that gets kids attention. It can be the source of craft materials for a really fun project. Or it can be filled with things that are for you only when the kids are asleep.

○ **Sitter's Notebook or tablet** to keep notes in and something to write with

○ **Books** to read to the children

○ **Video or DVD** to watch with the children

○ **Craft items, such as felt pieces, construction paper, foam shapes.** Be sure whatever you take is easy to clean up so you don't leave behind a mess for the parents. So leave the paint, glitter, glue, and other potential mess-makers at home.

○ **Deck of cards** to play "Go Fish" with the children or "Solitaire" by yourself

○ **Books for you** to read

○ **Your homework**

○ **Cell phone**

○ **A snack for you** (just in case)

○ **Little flashlight** (again, just in case)

○ **Sweater or jacket** (should their house be cool)

General Information

Family name:

Address:

Major cross streets:

Home phone number:

Names and ages of children:

name	age
name	age
name	age
name	age
name	age
name	age
name	age

Medical conditions, medications, or allergies

Foods not allowed:

_____

_____

_____

_____

Activities not allowed:

_____

_____

_____

_____

Father's name: _____

    phone number at work: _____

    cell phone: _____

Mother's name: _____

    phone number at work: _____

    cell phone: _____

Emergency Information

A relative, neighbor, or close friend to call:

home phone number:

cell phone:

Pediatrician:

office number:

emergency number:

Fire:

Police:

Ambulance:

Hospital:

Poison hotline:

All-purpose emergency number:

Other numbers:

(_____):
　　name

　　　number
(_____):
　　name

　　　number
(_____):
　　name

　　　number
(_____):
　　name

　　　number

Location of first aid kit:

_____

Location of fire extinguisher:

_____

Location of keys for interior doors:

_____

Journal Information

Kids' names, ages, and favorites or preferences:

Rules about food:

Times, rules, and routines for bed:

Bedtime stories and prayers:

Rules about homework:

_____

_____

_____

_____

Chores:

_____

_____

_____

Rules for use of TV, computer, appliances, and other equipment:

_____

_____

_____

Other special rules and instructions:

_____

_____

_____

_____

WHiLe we're Gone TODaY

Date: _____ Where we'll be: _____

How we can be reached there:

_____

alternate number:

_____

When we expect to be home:

_____

Medications to be given:

(Please write down child's name, medication name, dosage, schedule, and any special instructions. Sign instructions after sitter reads them aloud to verbally confirm.)

_____

_____

_____

_____

_____

_____
(parent signature)   (date)

Special instructions:

_____

_____

_____

_____

Sitter's Report

Rules and Discipline

I noticed these good behaviors:

Discipline was used for:

Calls

Who: _____ When: _____

Message:

Who: _____ When: _____

Message:

Who: _____ When: _____

Message:

Oops

Spills or other accidents:

Oowies

What happened and what I did:

Medications

Type:

Amount:

Time:

Playtime

We played these games:

We watched these shows:

Mealtime

What we ate:

When we ate:

All the rest (and how it went)

Naptime:

Bedtime:

Bathtime:

Bathroom breaks:

Comments

A prayer for You

God, You've called me to serve You
By watching over some of Your children.
Help me take this calling seriously.
Give me all those things I'll need to do it well—
Patience, kindness, cheerfulness, wisdom,
A true sense of responsibility, and humor.
Be with me during the good times
And during the hard times.
Guide me, support me, and use me as You will.
God, bless the children.
God, bless me.
In Jesus' name. Amen.